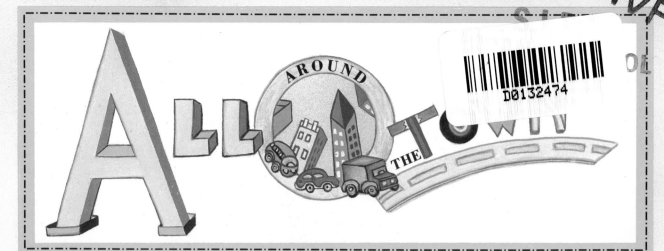

The Number of Players

2-4

The Object of the Game

To move from home at one end of the town to school at the other end of the town.

The Playing Pieces

One pair of dice and a different type of playing piece for each player: for example, a coin or a button.

The Play

Players take turns throwing the dice and subtracting the lesser number from the greater number. The player moves the playing piece forward to the nearest number that shows the subtraction difference. The game board includes penalty and bonus spaces. Players may occupy the same space.

The Winner

To win, a player's last roll must result in an odd-numbered answer.

Math Concepts

Determining greater and lesser numbers.
Subtracting numbers up to six.

I LOVE MATH

LOOK BOTH WAYS

CITY MATH

TIME
LIFE *for*
Children ™

ALEXANDRIA, VIRGINIA

ALL ABOUT
I LOVE MATH

Dear Parent,

The *I Love Math* series shows children that math is all around them in everything they do. It can be found at the grocery store, at a soccer game, in the kitchen, at the zoo, even in their own bodies. As you collect this series, each book will fill in another piece of your child's world, showing how math is a natural part of everyday activities.

Who else is on this bus? Find out on page 34.

What Is Math?

Math is much more than manipulating numbers; the goal of math education today is to help children become problem solvers. This means teaching kids to observe the world around them by looking for patterns and relationships, estimating, measuring, comparing, and using reasoning skills. From an early age, children do this naturally. They divide up cookies to share with friends, recognize shapes in pizza, measure how tall they have grown, or match colors and patterns as they dress themselves. Young children love math. But when math only takes the form of abstract formulas on worksheets, children begin to dislike it. The *I Love Math* series is designed to keep math natural and appealing.

How Do Children Learn Math?

Research has shown that children learn best by doing. Therefore, *I Love Math* is a hands-on, interactive learning experience. The math concepts are woven into stories in which entertaining characters invite your child to help them solve math challenges. Activities reinforce the concepts, and parent notes offer ways you and your child can have more fun with this program.

Follow the map on page 38 to tell me how I get home from school.

We have worked closely with math educators to include in these books a full range of math skills. As the series progresses, repetition of these skills in different formats will help your child master the basics of mathematical thinking.

What Will You Find in *City Math*?
In *City Math* your child will discover amazing shapes and patterns in the buildings and other structures of a city. He or she will also follow a map to find hidden treasure; use coordinates to locate silly goings-on in an apartment building; figure out a number pattern to solve a mystery about missing building addresses; and calculate how much it costs to park at a meter.

We hope *City Math* encourages you and your child to take a closer look at the shapes and patterns around you the next time you walk through a city or town together. Look up, look down, look all around. You will discover that the city is full of mathematical surprises, leading you to say:

I LOVE MATH!

**The Editors
Time-Life for Children**

Guess what we're waiting in line for. Read the story that begins on page 20.

Table of Contents

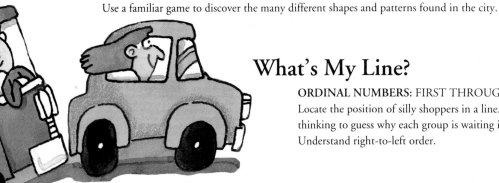

THE GREAT MAIL MIX-UP

Professor Guesser returned to her office carrying a Smellie's Deli sardine sandwich for lunch. But she couldn't get in the door. The mailmoose and three painters were blocking her way and having a terrible argument. "Excuse me," she interrupted. "Is there a problem?"

"We painted all the buildings on this side of the street," began Harry.

"We didn't want to get paint on the shiny building numbers," continued Tina.

"So I took them off and put them in this box," said Big Al.

My first day on the job and this had to happen. I can't deliver the mail when all the building numbers are missing!

MATH FOCUS: ODD AND EVEN NUMBERS.
Children learn a real-world application of odd and even numbers by recognizing the pattern in building addresses.

6

MORE FUN. Use buttons or other small objects to show even and odd numbers from 1 to 10. Have your child place the buttons side by side on a piece of paper in even groups: two buttons, four buttons, and so on up to ten buttons. He or she can then do the same with odd-numbered groups of buttons.

"Street numbers follow a pattern. We need to figure out the pattern on this street," said Professor Guesser.

"Look at the other side of the street," said Tina.

"That's odd," said the mailmoose.

"It is odd!" laughed Professor Guesser. "Hot diggity dog! I can see a number pattern, can you?"

"On one side of the street," said Big Al, "the numbers are 1, 3, 5, and—" Big Al stopped. "Wait a minute! There's no number on the library. But I think I know what that number must be. The pattern starts with 1 and skips every other number."

"Yes," said Professor Guesser. "Only odd numbers are on that side of the street. Now I know where the numbers you put in the box should go."

What number patterns do you see?

Can you figure out the street number for the library? Here's a hint: Look at the first three street numbers. What number comes next?

9

Which number goes on each building?

"Oh, I get it!" exclaimed the mailmoose. "All the numbers on one side of the street are odd numbers—1, 3, 5, 7, and 9. Your address is 2, so all the numbers on your side of the street must be even numbers."

"Hooray!" shouted the mailmoose. "My problem is solved. Thank you, professor."

Big Al followed the pattern and hammered all the building numbers back into place. The mailmoose delivered the mail, and Professor Guesser went back to her office and ate her delicious sardine submarine sandwich.

I've got your number
MAKE A MODEL OF YOUR STREET

1. Fold a piece of paper into thirds. Draw a line along each fold.

2. Pretend that the middle third is the road in front of your house. Color it black.

3. Draw five buildings along the top third of your paper. Write your house number on the front door of the middle building. Write the numbers on the front doors of the two buildings to the left of your house and on the front doors of the two buildings to the right of your house.

4. Turn the paper upside down. Draw five buildings along this third of your paper. On the front doors, write the numbers on the front doors of five buildings across the street from your house.

5. Fold the sides so the houses face each other across the street.

MATH FOCUS: ODD AND EVEN NUMBERS. Take a walk along your street to look at the house numbers before you do this activity. If you live on a circle or cul-de-sac, or on a road with few houses, you can choose another street.

MORE FUN. Lay out number cards in sequence: for example, playing cards from 2 through 10. Remove a few cards, show the remaining cards to your child, and ask him or her to name the missing cards. You can also ask your child to tell whether each missing card is odd or even.

What's Missing?

What color cat is missing?

Something is missing in each of these pictures. Can you find the pattern in each picture and tell what's missing?

PIZZA ICE CREAM GLASSES PIZZA ICE CREAM GLASSES ICE CREAM GLASSES

What's the missing store sign?

MATH FOCUS: PATTERNS. By recognizing and describing patterns, children learn to classify and organize information.

Help your child identify the "core" or repeating part of each pattern: for example, black cat; orange cat. Then help your child figure out what's missing in each scene.

MORE FUN. Have your child extend each pattern by telling the next three objects or numbers: for example, the next three taxi numbers would be 70, 80, and 90.

MATH FOCUS: GEOMETRY AND PATTERNS. By looking at pictures of buildings, children see how geometric shapes and patterns are used in the world around them.

Help your child describe the structure in each photograph and tell which one is his or her favorite.

WHAT'S MY LINE?

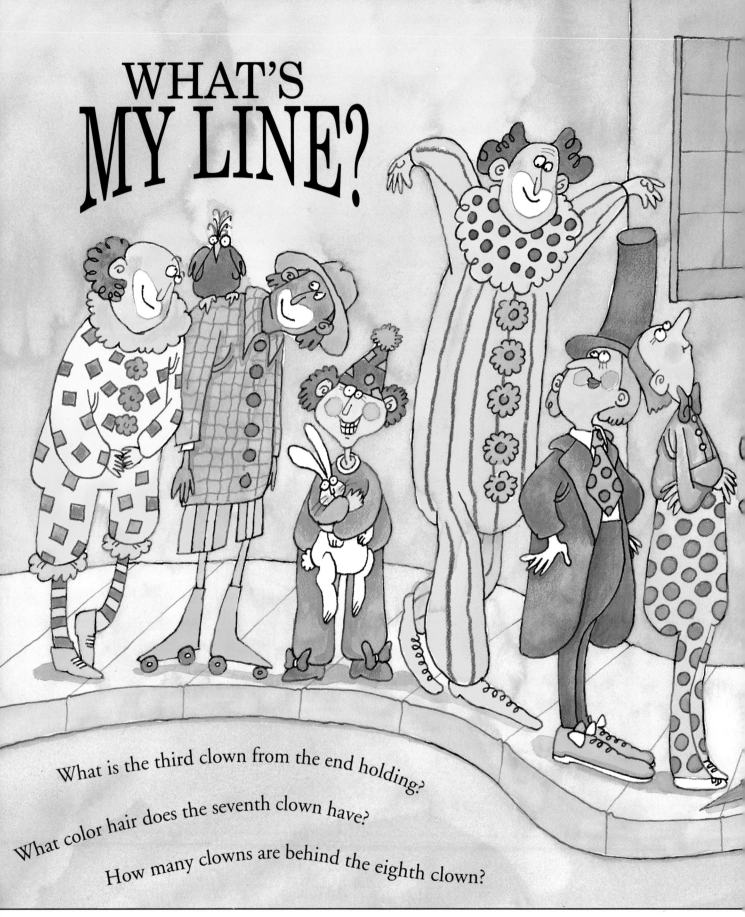

What is the third clown from the end holding?

What color hair does the seventh clown have?

How many clowns are behind the eighth clown?

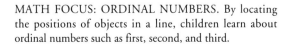

MATH FOCUS: ORDINAL NUMBERS. By locating the positions of objects in a line, children learn about ordinal numbers such as first, second, and third.

Before turning each page, have your child use the clues to figure out what the people are waiting in line for.

20

MORE FUN. Help your child cut out pictures of animals and people from magazines and glue them in a line on a piece of paper. Use ordinal numbers to ask position questions about the people and animals in the line.

21

Is the vehicle in front of the fourth one a truck?

Is the woman with orange hair in the tenth vehicle?

What color is the last vehicle in line?

22

What color hat is the driver of the third vehicle wearing?

How many vehicles are behind the sixth one?

Which vehicle in line has a clown in it?

How many vehicles are there altogether?

23

What color hair does the person in front of the eleventh person have?

How many people are in front of the seventh one?

In what place in line is the person wearing the roller skates?

Is the tenth person in line taller or shorter than the ninth person in line?

How many people are behind the second person?

Where in line is the person wearing a back pack?

What is around the neck of the one who is last in line?

25

SERRANO SCHOOL
24100 DELPHINIUM AVENUE.
MORENO VALLEY, CA 9238

Take a good look at this picture. The sneaker is first in line, isn't it?
What kind of shoe is second? Look closely and remember which shoe is where.
Then cover the shoes with your hands or a piece of paper.
What kind of shoe is in fourth place? What kind of shoe is in last place?
In which place is the roller skate?
Uncover the shoes.

Now look at this picture. The doll is first in line here.
Cover the toys. What kind of toy is fifth?
What kind of toy is third? In which place is the toy duck?
Uncover the toys.

Get five objects and put them in line. Play "Cover-Up" with a partner.
You can cover up the objects with a towel or a newspaper.

MATH FOCUS: ORDINAL NUMBERS. You can use this activity to help your child see the relationship between the ordinal numbers first through fifth and the cardinal numbers one through five.

MORE FUN. Try doing this activity with seven or eight objects.

MATH FOCUS: COORDINATE GRIDS. By describing the position of a point on a grid, children learn to use coordinates.

Help your child follow the dot's directions and answer the riddles.

MORE FUN. On pages 32 and 33, ask your child to choose a window and give its coordinates for you to find: for example, *over 2, up 3*. Once you've found the window, describe it to find out if it's the one your child chose. Take turns giving coordinates and finding windows.

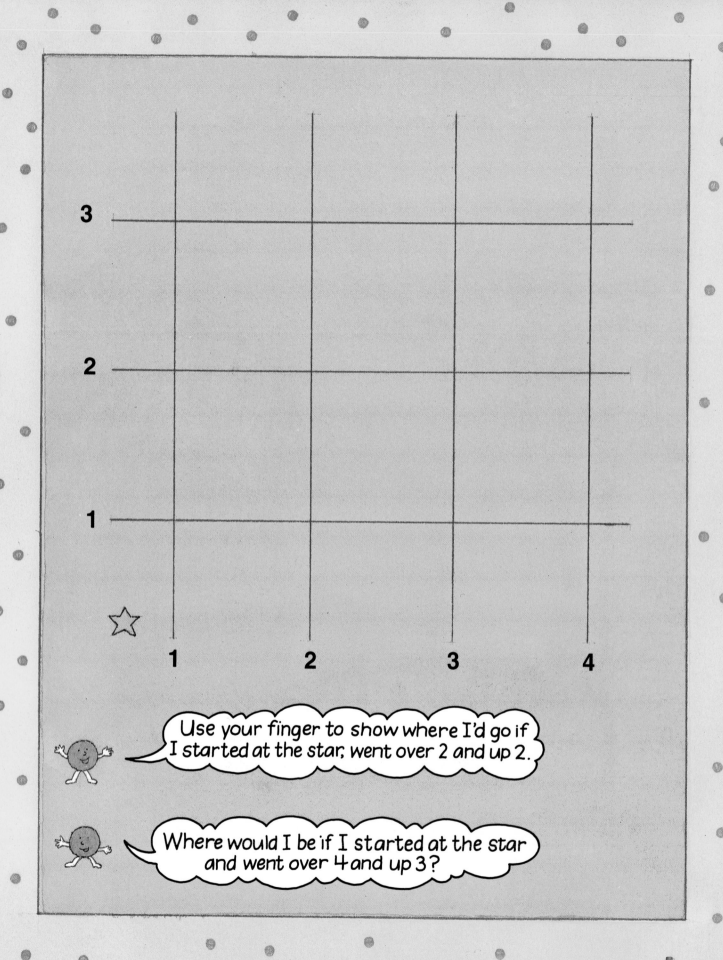

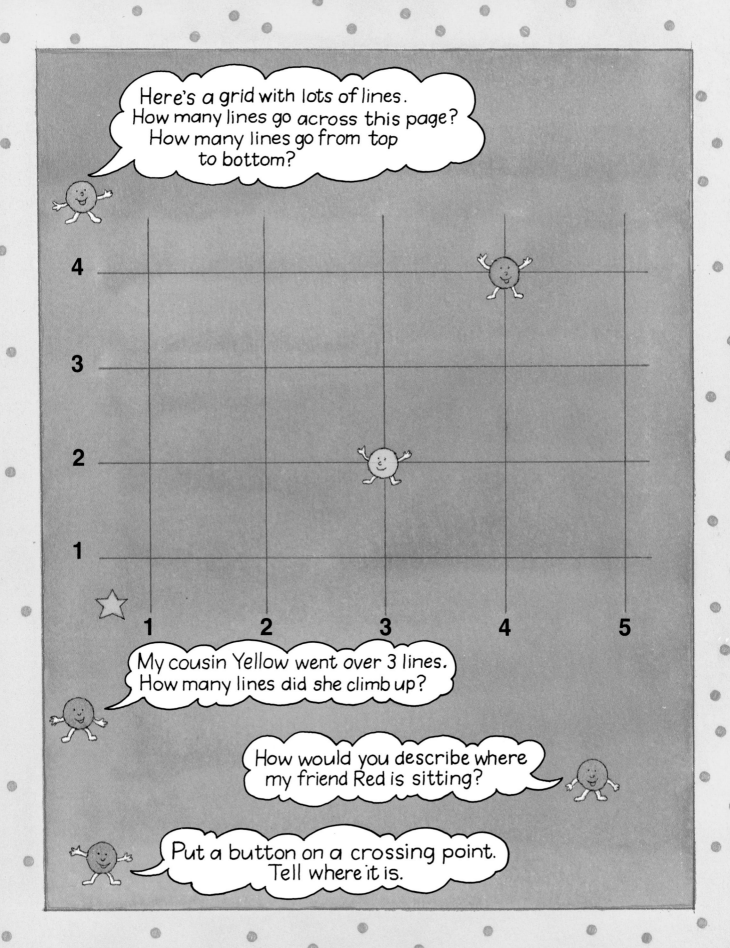

These riddles are about some silly things that are happening in this apartment building. To solve the first four riddles, put your finger on the star and count the number of windows over. Then, counting that window as number 1, count the number of windows up. For example, if you go over 3 and up 1 you will find the woman buying flowers. To solve the last two riddles, put your finger on the window being described. Then count over and up from the star.

Count over 2 windows, then up 1.
Who's at her desk having lots of fun?

Go over 4 windows. Now go up 3.
Something's hanging on the door.
What can it be?

Count over 4 windows, then up 1.
Who is trying a new dress on?

Go over 1 window, then up 3.
Who's at the table eating this great feast?

People in their living room watching TV.
Count over, then up; oh, where can they be?

A DOG on the fiddle? Look for the pup.
How many windows over and up?

START
HERE

Can you find my dot friends in this building? Tell me what color they are and how to find them.

32

2 3 4

How does Gus count people on the bus?

> *Tip: You can use coins or buttons to help you keep track of how many people get on and off the bus.*

At each stop, it's up to Gus
To count the people on his bus.

You can help him with the facts.
You might add, you might subtract.

Will you help the driver Gus
And count the people on the bus?

At First Street, 2 baseball players
Got right on with the mayor.

On came a juggler at Second Street,
Juggling oranges, juicy and sweet.

"Thanks for helping," said driver Gus.
"How many people are on the bus?"

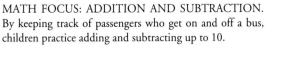

MATH FOCUS: ADDITION AND SUBTRACTION.
By keeping track of passengers who get on and off a bus,
children practice adding and subtracting up to 10.

34

Ask your child to "act out" the poem by using buttons or
coins to show passengers getting on and off the bus.
Remind your child not to count Gus the driver.

On Third Street, a girl and her mother
Got right on with gifts for each other.

At Fourth Street, 2 scuba divers
Stepped in behind a race-car driver.

At Fifth Street, 3 folks got out.
On stepped a judge and a tall Boy Scout.

"Thanks for helping," said driver Gus.
"How many people are on the bus?"

MORE FUN. Your child can create his or her own story or poem about passengers on a bus. Have your child use counters, such as buttons or coins, to act it out.

ANSWERS. Page 34: 4 people; page 35: 8 people; page 36: 6 people; page 37: 9 people.

At the Sixth Street stop, off stepped 6.
Then a builder got on, carrying bricks.

When Gus stopped at Seventh and Glen,
Onto the bus came 2 bearded men.

At the stop on busy Eighth Street,
Up stepped a boy with his pet named Pete.

"Thanks for helping," said driver Gus.
"How many people are on the bus?"

At the corner of Ninth, off went 3.
On came a girl with a bandaged knee.

Gus stopped his bus at noisy Tenth Street.
A band of 5 got on with a beat.

At Eleventh Street, Gus said with a shout,
"Last stop today! Everyone out."

"Thanks for helping," said driver Gus.
"How many people got off the bus?"

LOOK BOTH WAYS

Chip, Agatha, Arthur, and Pearl all go to the same school.

Every day at 3:00 they leave school and walk home.

Follow the colored footprints to see the route each child takes. The footprints match the colors of their sneakers.

Don't forget to look both ways when you cross a street.

MATH FOCUS: SPATIAL SENSE—TOPOGRAPHY (MAP DIRECTIONS). By using a map to solve problems, children develop their sense of the geometric relationships of objects in a given space.

MORE FUN. Have your child draw a simple map showing the path he or she takes to school or some other location.

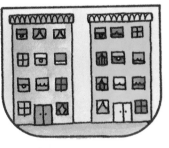

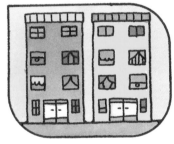

Who has the shortest walk home from school?

Can you see another way for Chip to get home from school?

Who walks past Arthur's house to get home?

Which children walk on Almond Way to get home?

Which way does Agatha turn onto 4th Street to get home?

Which children do not need to walk on Brazil Nut Blvd. to get home?

Who has the longest walk home?

Go to Avenue D and look for a building that has 4 square sides, a square roof, and a square floor. All 6 sides are the same size and shape. Add 1 plus 2 plus 3. On that floor, look on the bottom shelf for a white container with red speckles.

In a secret corner of the city, Mathman, champion of problem solvers everywhere, stood in front of his students on the last day of class. "You must pass one last test before you can be members of my Math Patrol," he said. "I have hidden a treasure in the city. Your test is to find it."

"How?" asked Adam.

"I will give you four clues. The first clue is written on the chalkboard. It will help you find the other clues," said Mathman, and he disappeared out the door with a hearty, "Go! Go! Math Patrol!"

"I've always wanted to go on a treasure hunt!" said Vanessa.

"Me too!" Adam agreed. "Let's get started. We have to go to Avenue D and look for a building that has 4 square sides, a square roof, and a square floor, with all 6 sides the same size and shape."

"Yeah—a cube," said Nina.

"Exactly," answered Adam.

"Where are we going to find a building that's a cube?" asked Vanessa.

"We know it must be somewhere on Avenue D," said Nina.

"I think I see it on the map," said Adam. "It's at the corner of 2nd Street and Avenue D."

Can you find the building that's a cube?

MATH FOCUS: LOGICAL THINKING, ADDITION, SUBTRACTION, SOLID SHAPES, ORDINAL NUMBERS, AND COORDINATE GRIDS. By solving clues, children learn to analyze information and to apply reasoning skills. Help your child solve each clue in the story before reading each answer.

41

MORE FUN. Your child may wish to hide a "treasure" somewhere in your home and challenge family members to find it by telling them a clue.

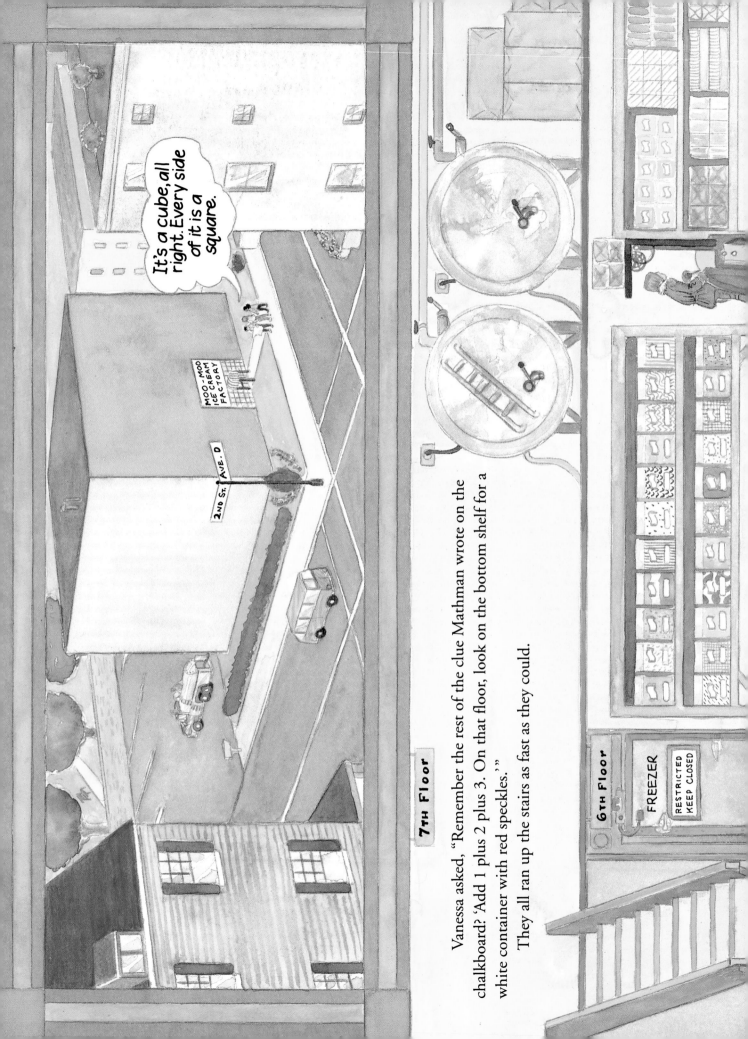

Vanessa asked, "Remember the rest of the clue Mathman wrote on the chalkboard? 'Add 1 plus 2 plus 3. On that floor, look on the bottom shelf for a white container with red speckles.'"

They all ran up the stairs as fast as they could.

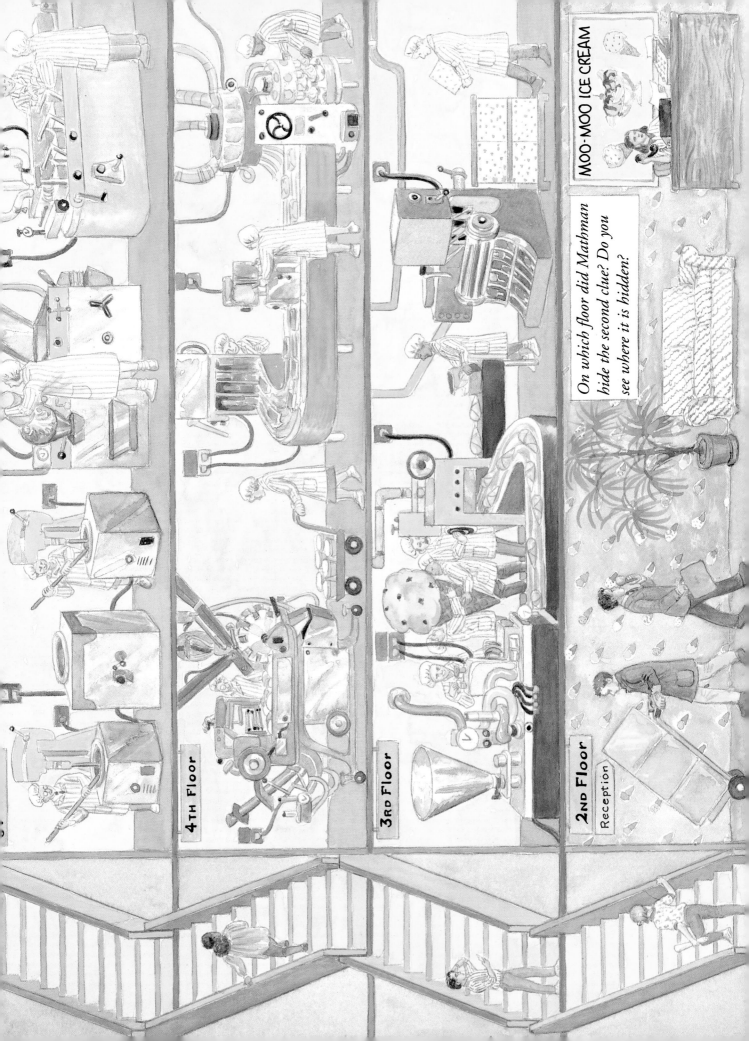

MOO-MOO ICE CREAM

On which floor did Mathman hide the second clue? Do you see where it is hidden?

4TH FLOOR

3RD FLOOR

2ND FLOOR
Reception

Nina read the first part of the clue to the others. "Go to 3rd Street and look for a building with a square floor and 4 sides made of triangles. The triangles come to a point at the top."

"The building's a pyramid, isn't it?" Vanessa asked as she opened the map.

"I think so," answered Adam.

Nina laughed. "Then it should be easy to find. There can't be too many pyramid-shaped buildings in town."

"There it is," said Vanessa, "at 3rd Street and Avenue C."

Can you find the pyramid?

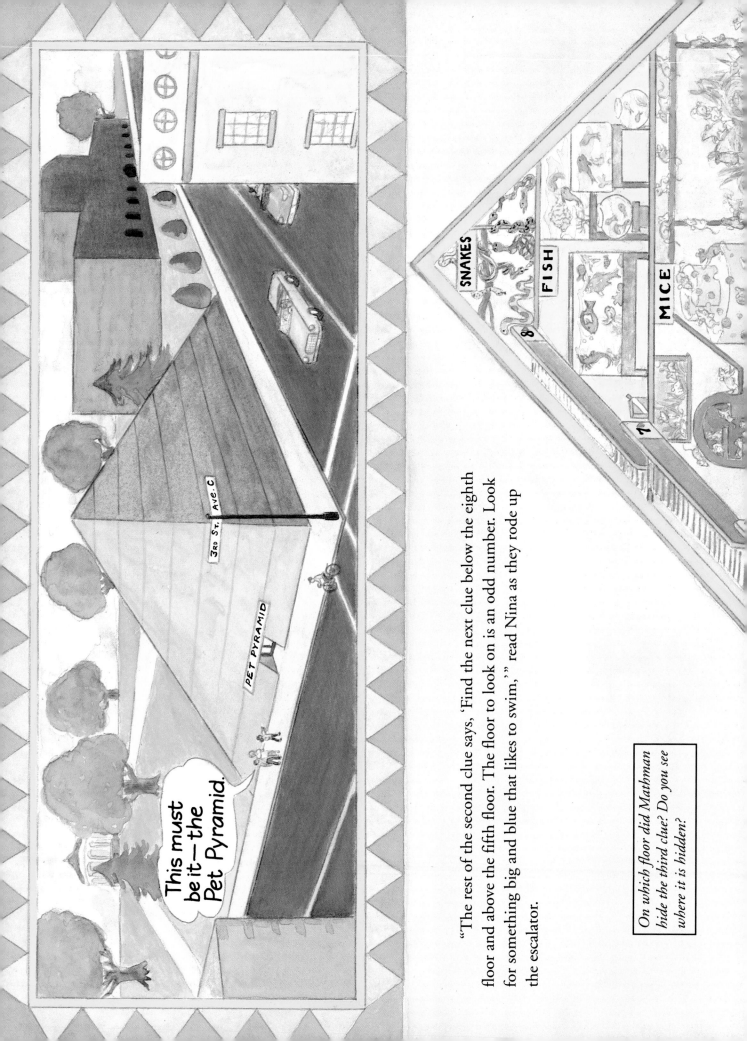

This must be it—the Pet Pyramid.

3RD ST.

AVE. C

PET PYRAMID

"The rest of the second clue says, 'Find the next clue below the eighth floor and above the fifth floor. The floor to look on is an odd number. Look for something big and blue that likes to swim,'" read Nina as they rode up the escalator.

SNAKES

FISH

MICE

On which floor did Mathman hide the third clue? Do you see where it is hidden?

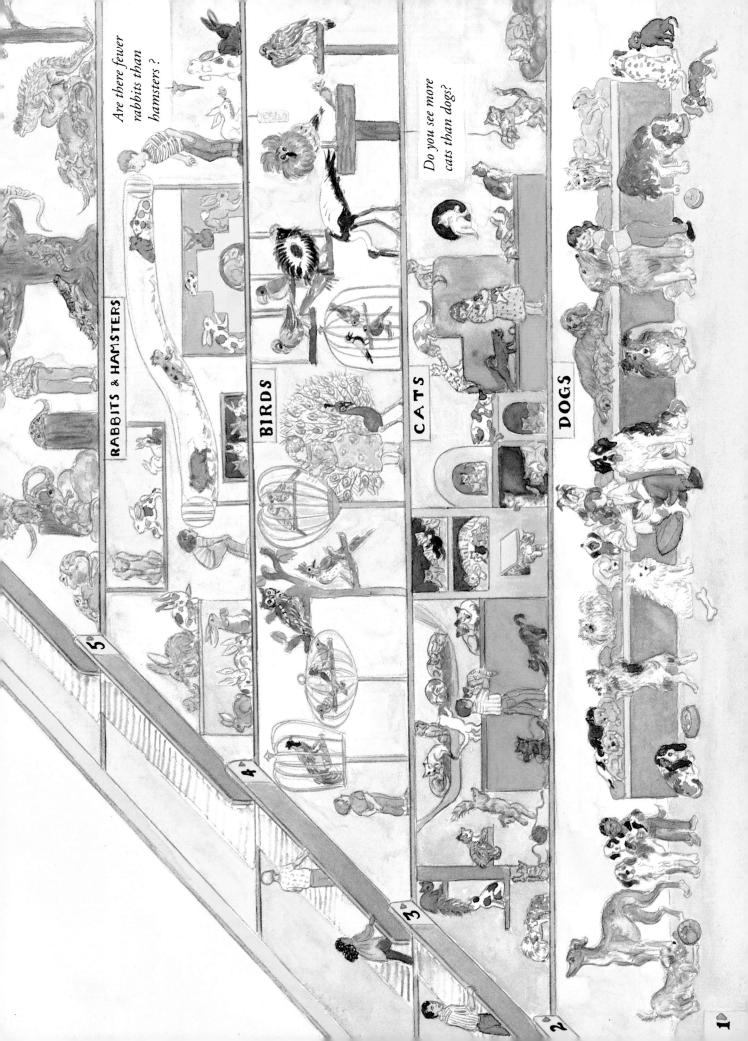

RABBITS & HAMSTERS

Are there fewer rabbits than hamsters?

BIRDS

CATS

Do you see more cats than dogs?

DOGS

1

2

3

4

5

Here's the clue!
I found it!

Adam read part of the clue aloud. "Look on Avenue B for a building that's round like a ball."

"Hmm. A ball-shaped building," Vanessa said. "It must be a sphere."

"I just hope it won't roll away before we get there," Nina added.

"Well, if it hasn't rolled away, it's on 2nd Street and Avenue B," said Adam.

Do you see the sphere-shaped building?

The students rushed to the museum. Adam read the rest of Mathman's third clue as they stepped into the elevator. "Count the number of students in your group, then add 2. The fourth clue is hidden on that floor in the mouth of a big green animal that flies."

Nina pressed the button for the correct floor and up they went!

SERRANO SCHOOL
24100 DELPHINIUM AVENUE
MORENO VALLEY, CA 9238

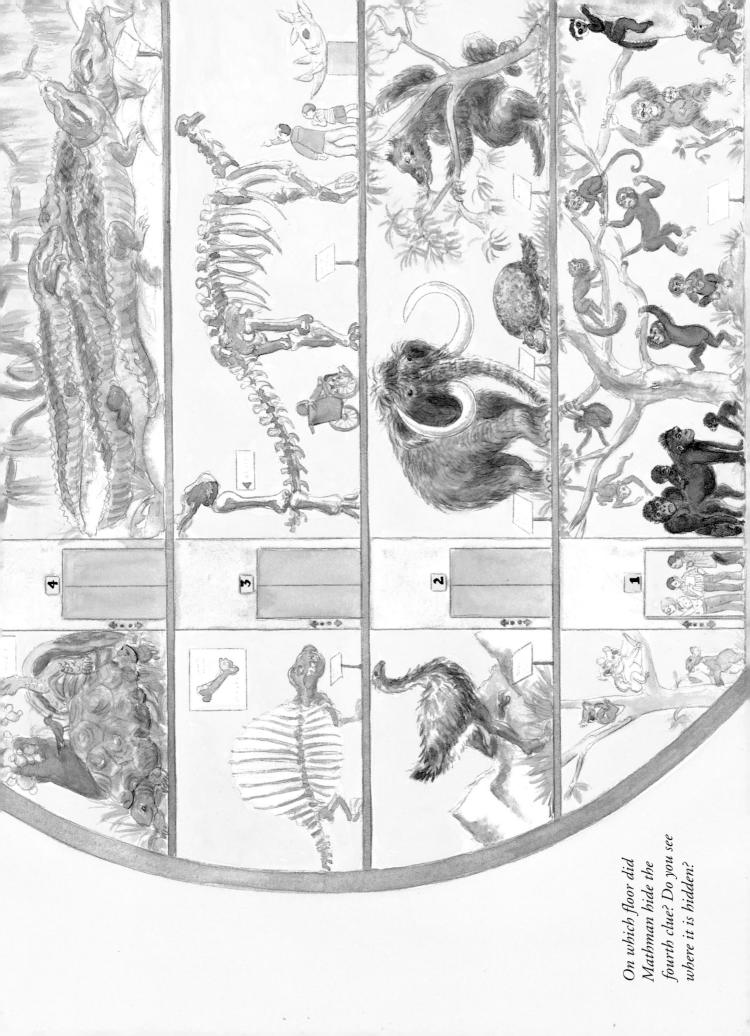

On which floor did Mathman hide the fourth clue? Do you see where it is hidden?

Do you see the building that is a rectangular prism?

Here's the clue! The pterodactyl's got it!

"Look on 4th Street. Find a building with a rectangle-shaped floor and roof, 2 rectangle-shaped sides, and 2 square sides," Vanessa read.

"That sounds like a rectangular prism," said Adam.

"Sounds like a stick of butter to me," replied Nina.

"Whatever it is, it's the building on the corner of 4th Street and Avenue B," Vanessa said.

They dashed into the Art Museum and looked around.

"The rest of this clue is strange," said Vanessa, as they hurried down the hall. "It says, 'You will see 4 doors close together. Enter the door that completes the number sentence $7 - 3 = \square$ and go down.'"

"Down?" asked Nina.

I've found the right room! The treasure at last!

The students pushed open the door and slid down into the basement.

"Hooray! You've done it!" shouted Mathman and the other Math Patrol members. Near them was a fancy trunk.

"Wow, a treasure chest!" Adam exclaimed. When the chest was opened, each student pulled out a new, official Math Patrol uniform, cape, and mask.

"These uniforms are treasures we'll wear with pride," Vanessa said.

"You've really earned them," said Mathman. "And you have an even greater treasure, too—being able to solve math problems like the ones in those clues. Now, all together:"

Go! Go! Math Patrol!

JUST BETWEEN YOU

between 1 and 10

between 11 and 20

between 21 and 30

between 31 and 40

between 41 and 50

My office number is 2. That's between 1 and 10. Look at the house numbers. Then use the numbers above to tell which two numbers each house number falls between.

17

6

34

42

73

MATH FOCUS: NUMBERS. By analyzing the sequence of numbers from 1 to 100, children gain an understanding of number order.

Have your child count out loud to help find the range for each house.

56

AND • ME

between
51 and 60

between
61 and 70

between
71 and 80

between
81 and 90

between
91 and 100

88

59

25

64

97

MORE FUN. Play "Just Between You and Me." Say a number and have your child identify the range of numbers it is between. Then change roles. You may

extend the game by saying the range of numbers and having your child say a number that falls within that range.

57

How Does Peter Feed The Meter?

HOURS 1 2 3 4 5 6 7 8 9
COST 10¢ 20¢ 30¢ 40¢ 50¢ 60¢ 70¢ 80¢ 90¢

When Peter drives into the city
and parks his shiny new jeep,
It costs Peter 10¢ an hour.
For parking, that's
certainly cheap!

Monday, Pete toured the museum
And saw oils by Vincent Van Gogh.
He parked his red jeep for 2 hours.
How much did it cost? Do you know?

Tuesday was spent watching baseball.
Some extra innings were played.
A 5-hour game start to finish.
How much for parking was paid?

Wednesday, Pete went to the opera.
A great prima donna was star.
He parked for 4 hours that evening.
How much did he pay for his car?

MATH FOCUS: MULTIPLICATION AND MONEY.
By adding equal amounts, children learn the relationship
between multiplication and addition.

58

Have available 30 dimes or use the dimes on this page.
Have your child count by tens to answer the questions in
the poem. He or she can use the parking meter on this
page to check the answers.

On Thursday, Pete drove to the city
To see a fantastic parade.
He parked for 3 hours at a meter.
How much money of Peter's was paid?

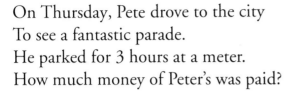

On Friday, at an outdoor concert,
Pete stayed till it got dark.
He listened and danced for 6 hours.
How much did it cost him to park?

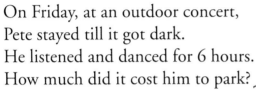

On Saturday, Pete went shopping.
He stayed in the city all day.
For 9 hours of continuous parking,
How much did Pete have to pay?

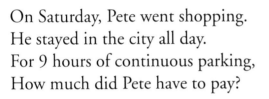

Sunday, Pete brought his new camera
To snap the view from a tower.
How much did it cost dizzy Peter
To park for exactly 1 hour?

Which day did parking cost the most money?
Which day did it cost the least?
How much did it cost altogether
For Peter to park his red jeep?

MORE FUN. Have you child pretend to be Peter and tell you what activities he or she would do in the city, how long the car would be parked, and how much it would cost to park.

ANSWERS. Parking cost Peter the most on Saturday. It cost him the least on Sunday. Peter paid $3 altogether.

Anytown, U.S.A.

Cathy, Bill, Lucy, and Carl all live in Anytown, U.S.A.
Use the clues to find out where each of them lives.

1. The shortest way for Lucy to get from her house to school
   is to pass the bowling alley and a yellow house. What color
   is Lucy's house? What else does Lucy pass on her way to school?

MATH FOCUS: LOGICAL THINKING. By using the
process of elimination to solve a problem, children learn to
use reasoning skills.

Each time a house is identified, have your child write the
name of the person who lives there on a piece of paper and
place it on that house.

2. When Cathy takes the shortest route from her house to the shoemaker's, she passes Carl's house, the ice-cream parlor, and the school. What color is Cathy's house? What else does she pass on her way to the shoemaker's?

3. What color is Carl's house? What color is Bill's house?

ANSWERS. 1. Lucy's house is green. Lucy also passes the pet shop, the shoemaker's, and the barber's. 2. Cathy's house is blue. Cathy also passes the barber's. 3. Carl's house is red. Bill's house is yellow.

Calculate It!

10 MILES

13 MILES

A

B

12 MILES

16 MILES

H

14 MILES

G

It's 10 miles from point Ⓐ to point Ⓑ.
How far is it from point Ⓑ to point Ⓒ?
How far would you travel if you went on route Ⓐ Ⓑ Ⓒ? You can use a calculator to find out.

Press 10   Press +
Press 13   Press =
The number on the display is the distance of route Ⓐ Ⓑ Ⓒ.

MATH FOCUS: ESTIMATION AND ADDITION. By guessing and then using the calculator to check distances, children practice estimating and adding.

Help your child press the calculator keys in the right order. Remind him or her to press the = key to get the answer.

62

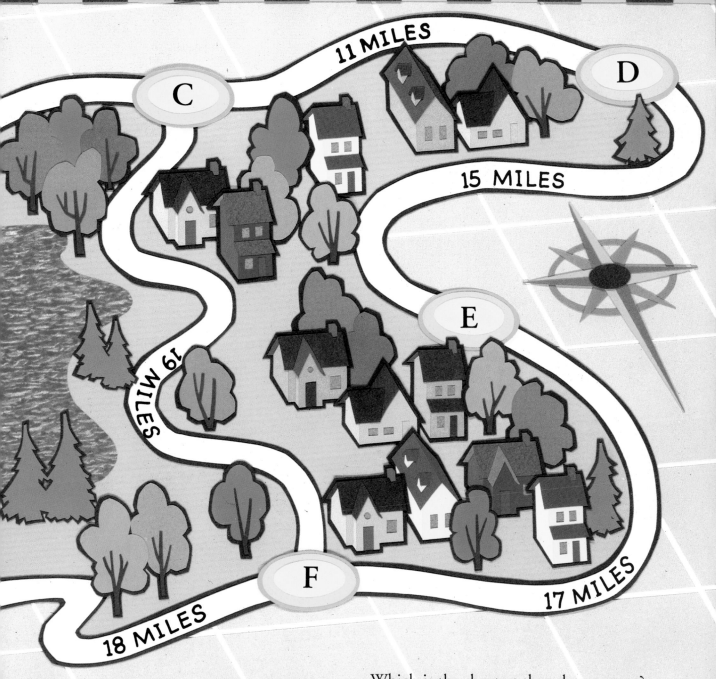

11 MILES

C

D

15 MILES

E

19 MILES

F

17 MILES

18 MILES

Now find the distances for each of
these routes.

Which is the shortest three-letter route?
Take a guess.
Then calculate it!

What is the shortest route from Ⓐ to Ⓕ?
Take a guess.
Then calculate it!

MORE FUN. Your child can calculate the distances
of routes with 4 points.

63

TIME-LIFE for CHILDREN™

Publisher: Robert H. Smith
Associate Publisher and Managing Editor: Neil Kagan
Assistant Managing Editor: Patricia Daniels
Editorial Directors: Jean Burke Crawford, Allan Fallow,
    Karin Kinney, Sara Mark, Elizabeth Ward
Director of Marketing: Margaret Mooney
Product Managers: Cassandra Ford,
    Shelley L. Schimkus
Director of Finance: Lisa Peterson
Financial Analyst: Patricia Vanderslice
Administrative Assistant: Barbara A. Jones
Production Manager: Prudence G. Harris
Production: Celia Beattie
Supervisor of Quality Control: James King

Produced by Kirchoff/Wohlberg, Inc.
866 United Nations Plaza,
New York, New York 10017

Series Director: Mary Jane Martin
Creative Director: Morris A. Kirchoff
Mathematics Director: Jo Dennis
Designer: Jessica A. Kirchoff
Assistant Designers: Brian Collins, Mariah Corrigan,
    Ann Eitzen, Judith Schwartz
Contributing Writers: Anne M. Miranda, Shereen Rutman
Managing Editor: Nancy Pernick
Editors: Susan M. Darwin, Beth Grout, David McCoy

CONSULTANTS

Mary Jane Martin spent 17 years working in elementary school classrooms as a teacher and reading consultant; for seven of those years she was a first-grade teacher. The second half of her career has been devoted to publishing. During this time she has helped create and produce a wide variety of innovative elementary programs, including two mathematics textbook series.

Jo Dennis has worked as a teacher and math consultant in England, Australia, and the United States for more than 20 years. Most recently, she has helped develop and write several mathematics textbooks for kindergarten, first grade, and second grade.

Catherine Motz Peterson is a curriculum specialist who spent five years developing an early elementary mathematics program for the nationally acclaimed Fairfax County Public Schools in Virginia. She is also mathematics consultant to the University Of Maryland, Catholic University, and the Fredrick County Public Schools in Maryland. Ms. Peterson is the director of the Capitol Hill Day School in Washington, D.C.

Cover Illustration: Lou Vaccaro

Illustration Credits: Liz Callen, pp. 20–26; Rosekrans Hoffman, pp. 60–61; Kathleen Howell, pp. 40–55; Jared Lee, pp. 34–37; Tom Leonard, p. 58; Don Madden, pp. 6–13, pp. 56–57; Frank McShane, pp. 62–63; Robin Oz, pp. 58–59; Judith Schwartz, front end papers; Lou Vaccaro, pp. 38–39; Joe Veno, pp. 16–19; Alexandra Wallner, pp. 14–15; Fred Winkowski, pp. 28–33

Photography Credits: Ken Biggs/TSW, pp. 16–17; Jacky Gucia/The Image Bank, p. 19*l*; David W. Hamilton/The Image Bank, p. 19*r*; Fritz Henle/Photo Researchers, p. 16*l*; Ken Karp/OPC, p. 27; J. Paul Kennedy/The Stock Market, pp. 16–17*b*; Michael Livenston/The Stock Market, pp. 18–19; George Loehr/The Image Bank, p. 18*r*; Peter Mauss/Esto Photographics, p. 16*r*; Joseph Nettis/Photo Researchers, back end papers; Jeff Spielman/The Image Bank, pp. 18–19*b*; John Stuart/The Image Bank, p. 17*r*; Wes Thompson/The Stock Market, p. 17*l*; David Weintraub/Photo Researchers, p. 18*l*

First printing. Printed in U.S.A.
Published simultaneously in Canada.

Time Life Inc. is a wholly owned subsidiary of THE TIME INC. BOOK COMPANY.

TIME-LIFE is a trademark of Time Warner Inc. U.S.A.

For subscription information, call 1-800-621-7026.

Library of Congress Cataloging-in-Publication Data

Look both ways: city math.
          p.   cm.—(I love math)
          Summary: A collection of stories, poems, riddles, games, and hands-on activities to develop early math skills by demonstrating how math is all around us in everything we do.
          ISBN 0-8094-9958-4
          1. Mathematics—Juvenile literature. [1. Mathematics. 2. Mathematical recreations.] I. Time-Life for Children (Firm). II. Series.
QA40.5.L66   1992
510—dc 20   92-25087
                                                          CIP
                                                          AC

THREE IN A ROW

The N

The C ters in a
row u

The ters
(butt

The ayer
tosses lace
his or dice
show and
up lines
and If a
co that
pla other
po nters
on nate
tu

Th hree
co

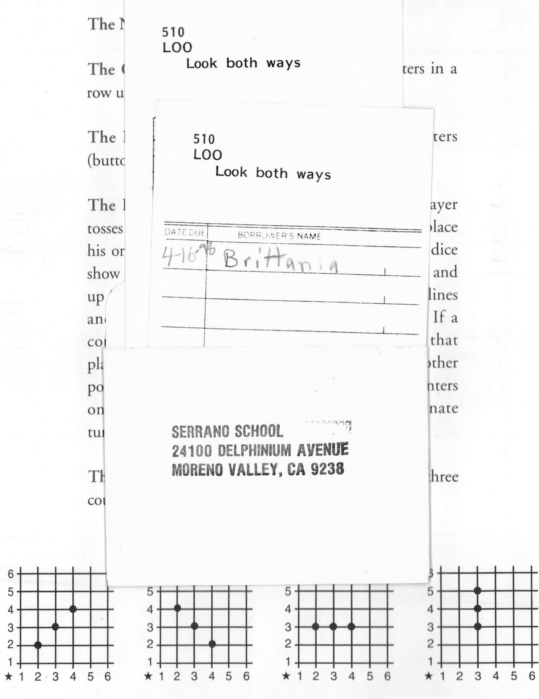

510
LOO
Look both ways

Math Concepts: Location of points on a coordinate grid.